My Truck

T0069729

Rebecca Sabatani

Illustrated by Gaston Vanzet

This is my truck.

I load my truck every day.

I drive my truck every day.

I unload my truck every day.

MARKET

I clean my truck every day.

I like my truck!